THE AMAZING

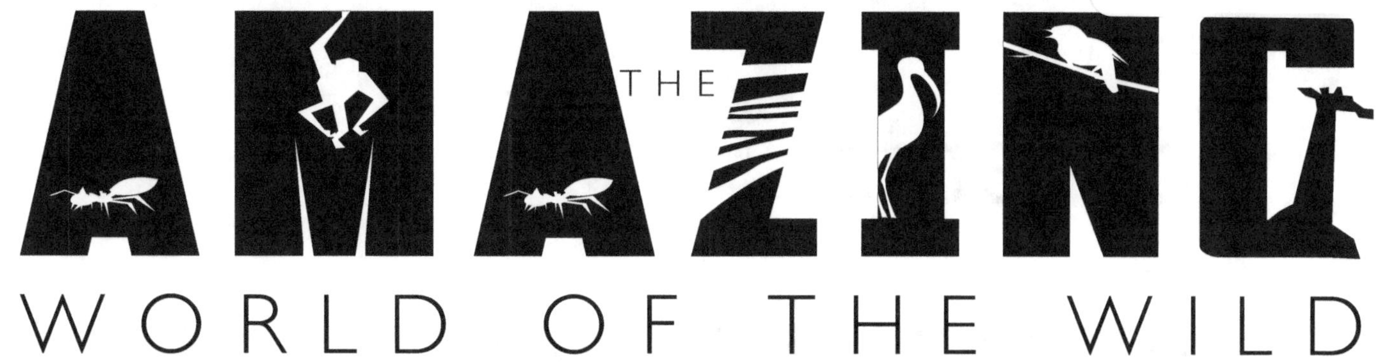

WORLD OF THE WILD

A SERIES OF BOOKS ABOUT THE WILD
VOLUME 1: NORTH AMERICA

INSECTS, BIRDS, FISH, AMPHIBIANS,
REPTILES, MAMMALS, AND OTHER INHABITANTS IN THEIR NATURAL ENVIRONMENT

NORTH AMERICA

PROVIDED ARE ILLUSTRATIONS, QUESTIONS AND EXERCISES THAT ARE CREATED
FROM THE EDUCATIONAL DISCOVERIES WITHIN THIS HANDBOOK. THESE ACTIVITIES
ARE FORMULATED FOR CHILDREN 8-12 YEARS OLD

START >>>

Contents

Around us are a large variety of animals. They range from being so small that you cannot see them to being as big as a house! Scientists divide the animals into groups. The most common groups are insects, fish, amphibians, reptiles, birds, and mammals. It should be noted that animals cannot create nutrients themselves like plants do by using sunlight, therefore, they need different types of food. Plant eating animals are called herbivores while animals that consume. Animals that consume other animals are called predators or carnivores, even though predators are known for eating meat, there are a lot of them that don't mind eating delicious fruits too. So, get ready, grab your tools, and let's go! Together, we are going to dive deep and discover the mysteries of this amazing world of the wild...

Insects

Insects are one of the oldest creatures on Earth. Insects can be found everywhere including the desert, the tundra, in the air, on the ground, in the soil, and under water. Scientists who study insects are called Entomologists, and they say that approximately one million different insect species have been scientifically discovered. They also say that researchers will be able to add the another million to the list in the future. During dozens of expeditions, hundreds of people are looking for new types of insects. Is it worth spending such an effort to study some of the bugs? No doubt! In nature, there are a huge number of insects that are helpful to people.

For example, bees give us honey, wax, and other products. Silkworms produce cocoons that are naturally made of silk which is the same silk we get some of our fabrics from. Thousands and thousands of insects pollinate the flowering plants, without which there would be no vegetation on our planet. There are predatory insects that destroy the pests in the fields and in the woods. It is scientifically known that insects can be very important for both medicine and agriculture.

By the way, did you know that every little creature isn't considered an insect? For example, spiders are not insects; they are Arachnids. In order to be called an insect, it must have at least three pairs of legs and one or more pairs of wings.

- Questions:

  What are the scientists who study insects called?

  ____
  ____
  ____

  What do the bees give us?

  ____
  ____
  ____

  How many pairs of legs and how many pairs of wings should insects have?

  ____
  ____
  ____

- Draw here what you liked most about this chapter:

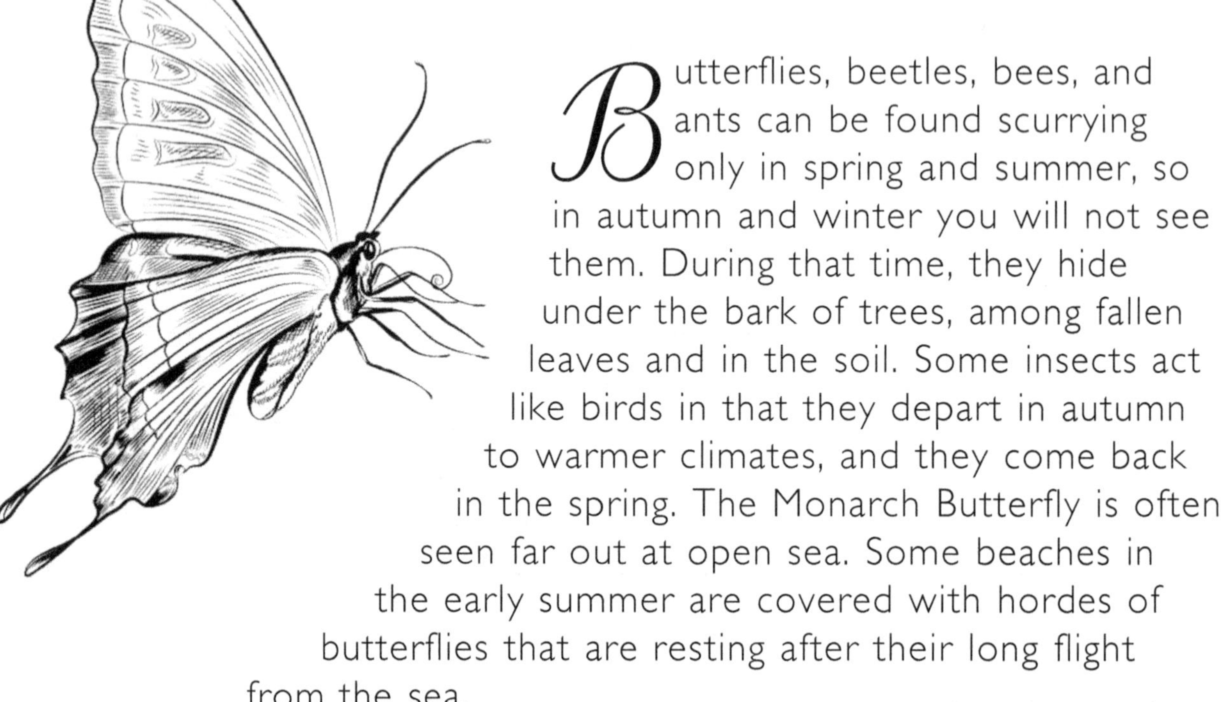

*B*utterflies, beetles, bees, and ants can be found scurrying only in spring and summer, so in autumn and winter you will not see them. During that time, they hide under the bark of trees, among fallen leaves and in the soil. Some insects act like birds in that they depart in autumn to warmer climates, and they come back in the spring. The Monarch Butterfly is often seen far out at open sea. Some beaches in the early summer are covered with hordes of butterflies that are resting after their long flight from the sea.

Most insects have three life stages: egg, larvae and adult. In the first stage, insects are found in eggs which then hatch into the second stage where they are called larvae. Once fully grown, they enter into their third stage of life, adulthood. Other insects, such as the butterfly, have four life stages instead of three: egg, larvae (caterpillar), pupa (cocoon), and adult (butterfly). After some time, the caterpillar will turn into a chrysalis. During the pupa stage, the caterpillar goes through a complete body change as it transforms into a butterfly. In due time, the shell of the pupa bursts and from it emerges the adult insect known as the butterfly. Even the really hairy caterpillar turns into a beautiful butterfly!

• Questions:

Where do the insects hide in autumn and winter?

____
____
____

What comes out of the insect's eggs?

____
____
____

What does a caterpillar become before turning into the butterfly?

____
____
____

• Draw here what you liked most about this chapter:

*I*nsects are called Arthropods because their feet consist of a certain number of rigid, interconnected parts. Insect life is full of dangers because they have many enemies. Many of them hide in nooks trying to camouflage (blend in) to their surroundings. The grasshopper is very difficult to see in the green grass, or some butterflies look similar to leaves or flowers, and some insects are impossible to discern from the bark of a tree.

The adolescent stage of life for some insects can last a very long time. The May Beetle larvae, for instance, develop for four years, whereas the larvae of houseflies take just a few days to mature. Not all insects' paths to adulthood are difficult. For example, the grasshopper does not happen thus. Emerging from the egg, the larva is similar to the adult insect. It grows and molts (discards its outer shell) several times until it finally becomes an adult grasshopper with wings.

- Questions:

  How long does it take for the eggs of a housefly to mature?

  ____

  ____

  ____

  Why are insects called Arthropods?

  ____

  ____

  ____

  Why does a grasshopper hide in the grass if there is danger?

  ____

  ____

  ____

- Draw here what you liked most about this chapter:

ometimes, insects can be cunning in the presence of danger by pretending to be dead. For example, a Bronze Beetle will not move if you touch it or its legs. You can twirl it in your hands to reveal its wings, but the beetle will not show any sign of life. This is how it protects itself from enemies. On the other hand, some insects act as if they are shouting as if to say, "Look, I'm here! Don't confuse me with someone else!" These insects are inedible, meaning they have a disgusting taste. After tasting them the first time, the predator never touches it again. Other insects, such as bees or hornets, have poisonous weapons known as stingers.

Of course, there are many insects that are harmful to man. They destroy the crops in the fields, or they eat the leaves of trees causing irreparable damage to forests. Mosquitoes and flies can ruin an entire country or torment grazing animals. Such insects often carry dangerous, infectious diseases.

You should know that in nature there isn't an insect that is absolutely harmful or unuseful. If you destroy all the mosquitoes, then some birds could die from hunger. In nature there is a balance, so the destruction of one species can lead to the extinction of others. People have learned to use some of the "harmful" insects to control weeds and other pests. Many insects are considered to be the ornaments of the meadows, fields and forests, and they enrich the world with colors, sounds and movements in nature all around us.

• Questions:

1. Which insects have a poisonous weapon?

____
____
____

2. How can insects be harmful to people?

____
____
____

3. What will happen if all of the mosquitos died?

____
____
____

• Draw here what you liked most about this chapter:

Test Yourself:

Let's check: how well do you know insects?
Write under each insect its name.

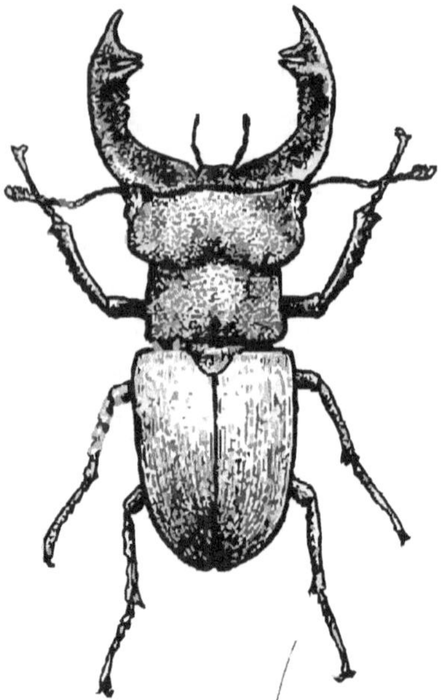

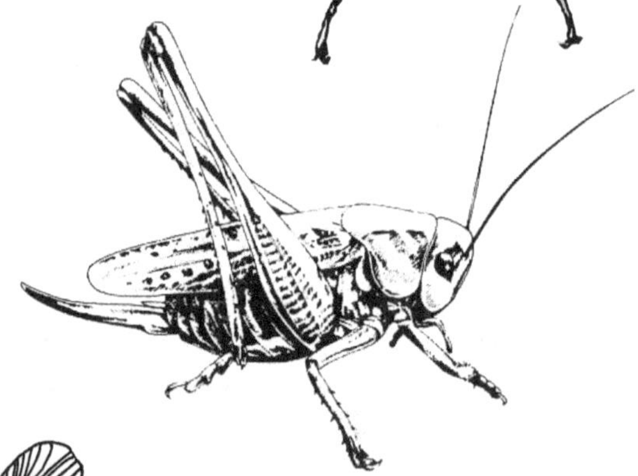

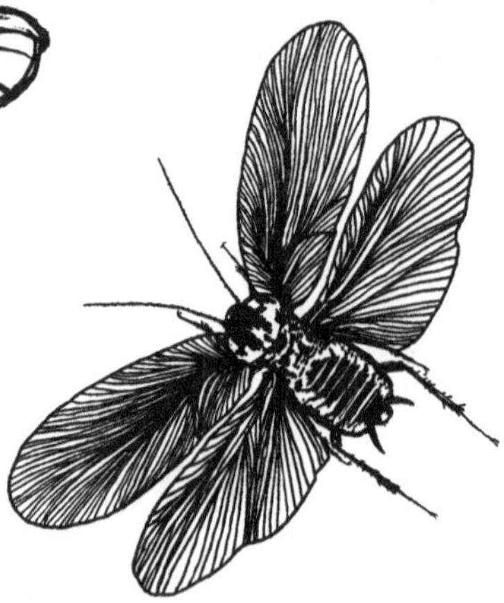

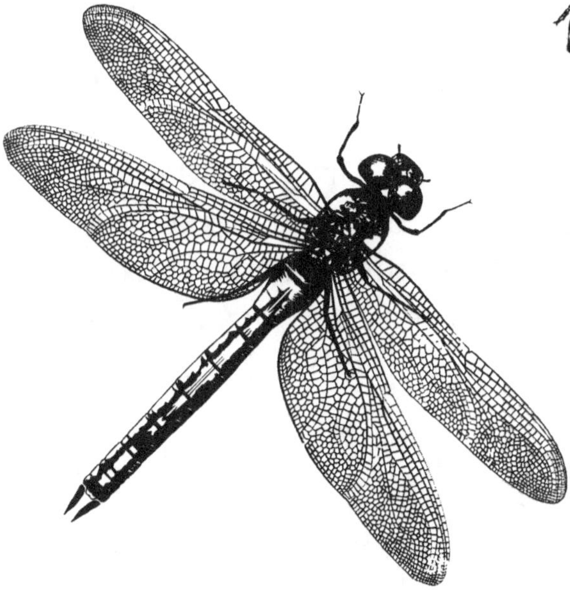

Fish

Did you know that near us is a huge world called the ocean? Its surface layer is a few hundred feet, so if someone wants to go deeper for scientific study, they must use a submarine. If a dive is more than a half a mile deep, the water will have a monstrous force of pressure which is a hundred times greater than air pressure. The deepest point in the ocean is called the Mariana Trench, and it is about seven miles deep. Scientists say that the depth of the seas and oceans studied are more mysterious than the depths of the universe!

Fish are very shy, so they only can be occasionally seen in small areas of water such as ponds, but if you crumble some bread in the shallow waters on a warm Summer day, you will see the young fish, also known as fry, attack the crumbs. Once they grow up and become adult fish, they prefer to escape into the depths of the water or into a kelp forest. Because of this, the easiest way to watch fish is in an aquarium where you can study their habits more easily or just admire them.

The body of the fish is covered with small, hard plates called scales. They protect the fish's body, and it doesn't interfere with its mobility because, in order to swim, the body is supposed to bend easily. The scales grow as the fish ages, so you can determine the fish's age by the lines on its surface just as you would count the annual rings on a tree to tell its age. Fish breathe by its gills, and they are arranged so that they can extract oxygen which then dissolves into the water.

- **Questions:**

  1. What is the special equipment for going to the bottom of the ocean called?

  ____

  ____

  ____

  2. What is a fish called before it becomes an adult fish?

  ____

  ____

  ____

  3. What do fish breathe with?

  ____

  ____

  ____

- **Draw here what you liked most about this chapter:**

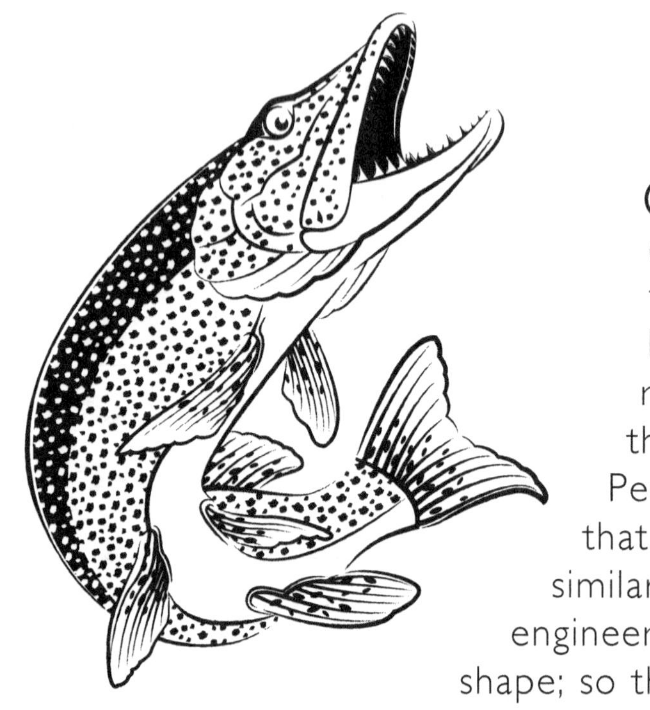

The fins and tail of the fish are what make them able to swim very fast. People discovered this secret, so in order to swim faster, they invented fins to put on people's feet and sometimes hands. Most fish have a smooth and rounded body shape which also allows them to swim quickly under water. People noticed this, so it is not a surprise that modern submarines are designed to be similar to giant fish. It's the same reason why engineers have given some cars a streamlined shape; so that it can develop more speed.

The coloration of fish is varied. Small fish hide from predators, so they try to be invisible against the background of surrounding objects. The predatory fish, in the same way, must be inconspicuous in an ambush in order to suddenly attack its prey without being detected. Fish that live among aquatic plants, such as Pike, have a dark green back and lighter sides with transverse dark stripes. Fish living in the upper layers of the reservoir have more of a silver color while a Flounder looks like a dirty, yellow plate so that it is difficult to distinguish between it and the sandy bottom.

• Questions:

1. What helps a fish to swim?

____

____

____

2. What did people invent to swim better?

____

____

____

3. What does a Flounder look like?

____

____

____

• Draw here what you liked most about this chapter:

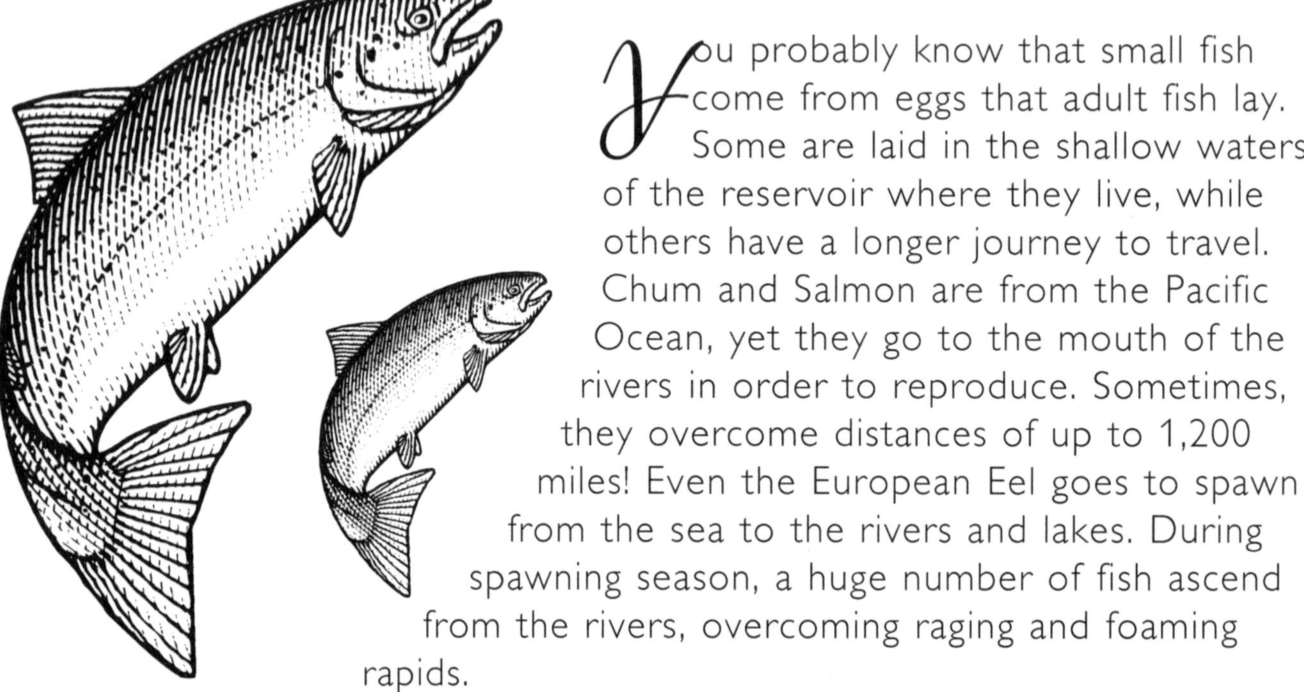

You probably know that small fish come from eggs that adult fish lay. Some are laid in the shallow waters of the reservoir where they live, while others have a longer journey to travel. Chum and Salmon are from the Pacific Ocean, yet they go to the mouth of the rivers in order to reproduce. Sometimes, they overcome distances of up to 1,200 miles! Even the European Eel goes to spawn from the sea to the rivers and lakes. During spawning season, a huge number of fish ascend from the rivers, overcoming raging and foaming rapids.

In the beginning when people were building hydropower plants that blocked rivers, they did not think about the effect it would have on the fish during spawning season, and that's why a lot of fish that stumbled upon such an obstacle died. Now, we have built these special shafts along these big walls so that the fish can safely and easily pass by.

Fish have a lot of enemies, and even their eggs are eaten by various animals, so in order for offspring to have a better chance of survival, the fish produce a lot of eggs known as caviar. For example, a female River Bass lays 200,000 to 300,000 eggs at a time while a female Cod will lay up to 10,000,000!

• Questions:

1. Where do baby fish come from?

2. Who makes the caviar?

3. How much caviar do fish make — a lot or a little?

• Draw here what you liked most about this chapter:

*H*ow does a fish survive the winter? It turns out that nature has arranged it so that near the bottom the temperature of the water never drops below forty degrees Fahrenheit. Believe it or not, the snow, ice and water actually protect them from the bitter cold. Even so, in winter the fish seem to be lazy and slow as if they are hibernating. This is because the fish are cold-blooded. Humans and many other animals are warm blooded, meaning that the blood helps keep the body warm during cold weather, but the temperature of the blood of fish is the same as the surrounding water. It lowers the temperature of the body which slows down the metabolic processes in the fish, and making the fish take on the appearance of being "lazy".

In the winter, fish are prone to another danger. The water is covered with ice, so there is not enough oxygen in the water for them to breathe. Sometimes, we drill holes in the ice so that the fish don't die of suffocation. Some fish sleep, or hibernate, by burying themselves in the mud while others swim toward the holes that are rich in oxygen.

• Questions:

   1. Why are fish not cold under water?

   ____

   ____

   ____

   2. Why do fish move so slowly in the winter?

   ____

   ____

   ____

   3. Why is there not enough oxygen for fish in winter?

   ____

   ____

   ____

• Draw here what you liked most about this chapter:

Test Yourself:

Let's check: how well do you know fish and other inhabitants?
Write under each sea inhabitant its name.

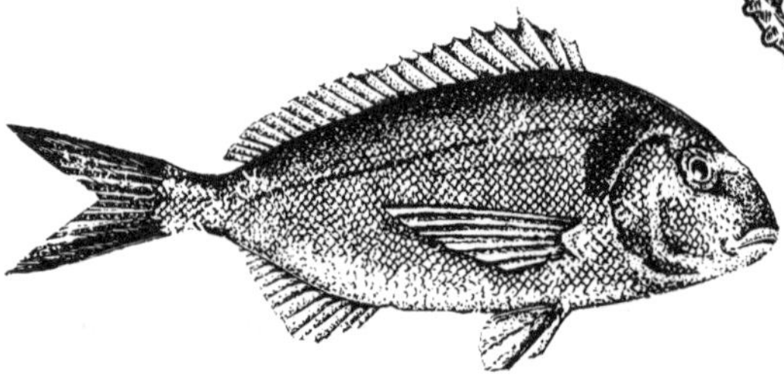

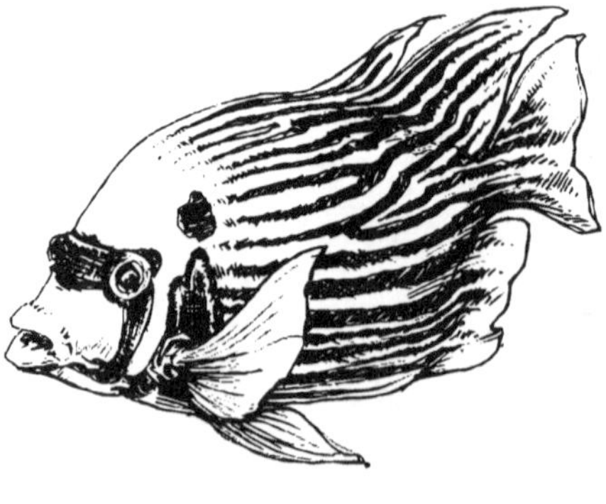

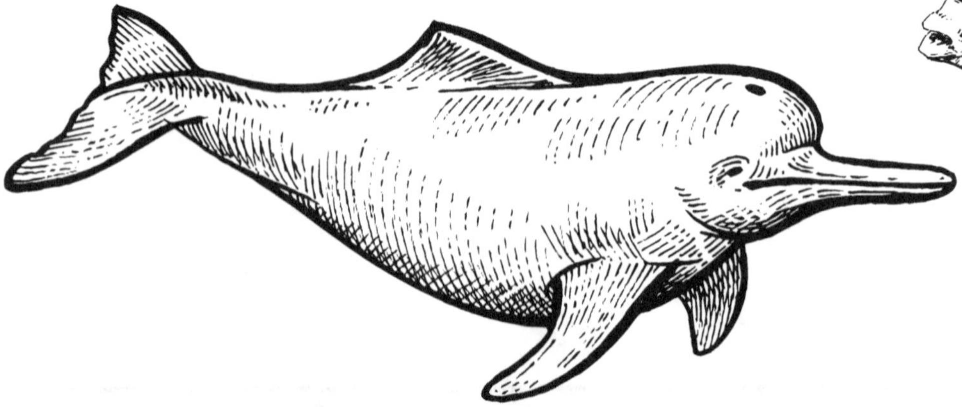

Amphibians

The name itself suggests that these animals can live both in water and on land. Usually, amphibians are found in fresh water and live close to it. You've probably seen frogs on the shore of a pond or a lake. If you approach them, they immediately escape by jumping into the water. In the spring and early summer in shallow, stagnant ponds live newts. In the rest of the year, they can be found in deciduous forests, parks and gardens. Some types of amphibians, such as the common frog or toad, live away from water. It's only during the breeding season that they move closer to the water.

Amphibians have lungs which allow them to live on land, but under the water, they breathe through their skin which is covered with a layer of mucus. The mucus dissolves into oxygen which is then absorbed into the bloodstream. In addition, the mucus neutralizes the skin from various pathogenic bacteria - tiny, invisible living creatures. The skin of some toads and salamanders emits toxic substances which protects them from enemies.

The toxins of amphibians that live in our area are too weak and do not harm humans, but toads that live in tropical forests have a poison that is fatal to us. It is because of the fatal toxicity of their skin that some Indian tribes soak the tips of their arrows using the toad's mucus as a way to make poisonous arrows.

• Questions:

1. Which amphibians can live far away from water?

____

____

____

2. How do amphibians breathe under water?

____

____

____

3. Where do the toads that have deadly poison live?

____

____

____

• Draw here what you liked most about this chapter:

Frogs typically live at the bottom of ponds during winter, but toads and newts live under driftwood or in abandoned animal burrows. After hibernation, all amphibians congregate in fresh water where they lay their eggs. You have probably seen in the water near the shore of ponds or even puddles large lumps of transparent droplets with black nucleoli. These are frog eggs. In about a week's time they hatch into larvae which are more like fish than frogs because they have gills and a tail. The larvae gradually change and grow their back legs first and then the front legs while the tail shrinks. During this stage of growth they are called tadpoles. After some time, the tadpole becomes a frog and is able to transition onto land.

In early spring, frogs and toads have little concerts on the banks of the ponds. The males try to attract the attention of the female frogs. In the southern regions, often in the evenings, you can hear them singing like a bird. It is often surprising to discover that the frogs that make these melodic sounds live on trees. These small frogs that are like little travelers. With the help of their suction cups, they attached themselves to the legs of migratory birds that descend to the water to rest. Like the passengers on a plane, they can travel hundreds of miles away. Amphibians eat many insect and pests of the fields and forests which are carriers of dangerous diseases to humans and animals. Toads do their hunting at night which is very important because they have to hide in the plants from predators during the day. This is very important because during the day they can only protect themselves from predators by hiding in the plants. It's not smart to kill the frogs because they eat mosquitoes and larvae of insects that grow in stagnant water. The more frogs in the area, the less we are annoyed by the mosquitoes.

- Questions:

    1. Where do amphibians lay their eggs?

    2. What are the differences between tadpoles and frogs?

    3. Why it is not smart to kill frogs?

- Draw here what you liked most about this chapter

Reptiles

You most likely have primarily seen these animals in books or movies. Although you may never encounter an alligator in the wild, it is highly possible that you may accidently disturb a snake hidden in the grass. Many reptiles like to bask in the sun on a wooden porch of a house or in the trunk of a tree. The body of a reptile is covered with scales, and it acts as a shield as it protects them while they crawl or slither around. Some reptiles, such as turtles, can hide in a solid shell in the presence of danger. In addition, the hard shell protects the body of the reptile from losing water. That is why these animals are able to live in waterless deserts.

The Sand Lizard prefers open, sunny places to live such as the edges of a forest, gardens, or forest clearings. Poisonous snakes can live in our areas too, and are responsible for more frequent human deaths in America than any other group of snakes. Most species are nocturnal, although some are found at higher altitudes and are active during the day. Otherwise, you can see them on cloudy days or during periods of rain. Most snakes are terrestrial, although some of them can live in the water. Snakes, like all cold-blooded animals, are active only during the warmer times of the day, and when the temperature is lower, they become lethargic or fall asleep. In winter, snakes slither their way into holes and go dormant. In the warmer the regions, there are more reptiles that live there. Many of them live among the loose sands of the deserts which is also where many turtles live.

- **Questions:**

1. What is a reptile's body covered with?

2. Where do the turtles hide in case of danger?

3. At what time of the day are snakes active?

- **Draw here what you liked most about this chapter:**

*A*lligator live in warm countries which is why they are active all year round. They spend most of their time in the water and hunt at night. Even the large animals going to the watering holes will sometimes become their prey. Sometimes, it may appear that reptiles cry, but this isn't the case. The "tears" from the reptiles are just a flow of excess salt. Small snakes, lizards, turtles and alligators are born from eggs that the mothers lay in the dirt and sand holes among the rocks or in piles of rotting leaves. Once hatched, they quickly grow and mature into adulthood.

You might ask yourself: "If snakes are that dangerous for people, why don't we just kill them all?" Well, there is balance in nature, and each group of animals has its own place. Take all the snakes away, and the balance will be ruined. For instance, who would keep the rats, which are usually eaten by snakes, from spreading? Rats and mice would destroy all of the harvests that are stored and still growing. Also, snake venom can be used in making pain killing medication and special sanitizers that stop bleeding. Turtles and lizards are very important too because they eat harmful bugs.

- **Questions:**

1. In what types countries do alligators dwell?

____
____
____

2. What is the "tears" from the reptiles?

____
____
____

3. What things can be made from the venom of snakes?

____
____
____

- **Draw here what you liked most about this chapter:**

Test Yourself:

Let's check: how well do you know amphibians and reptiles?
Write under each reptile its name.

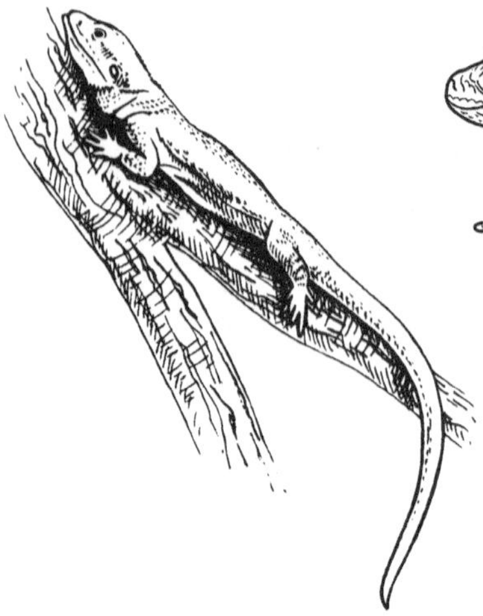
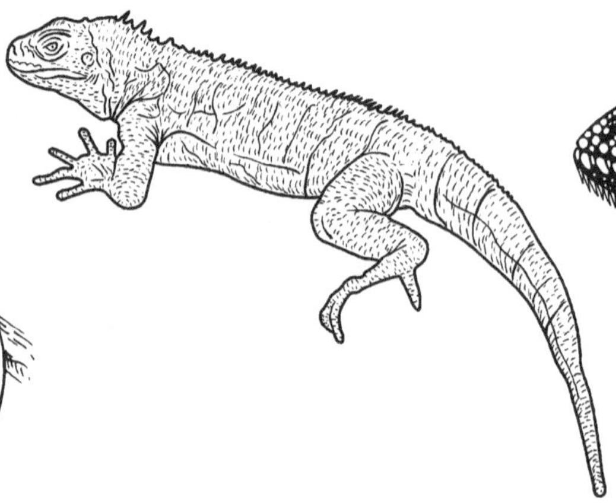
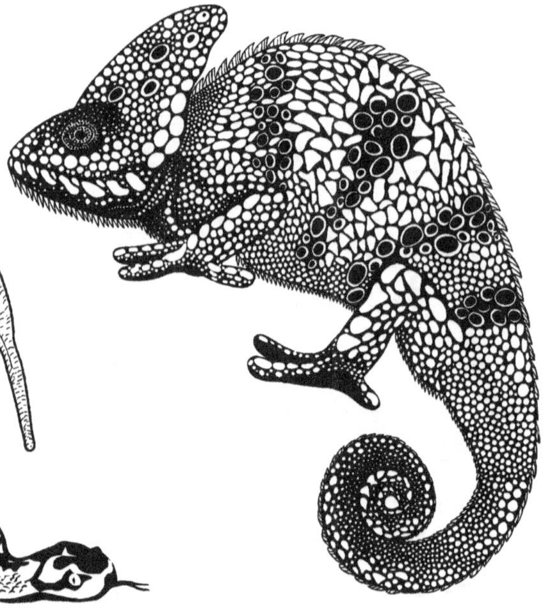
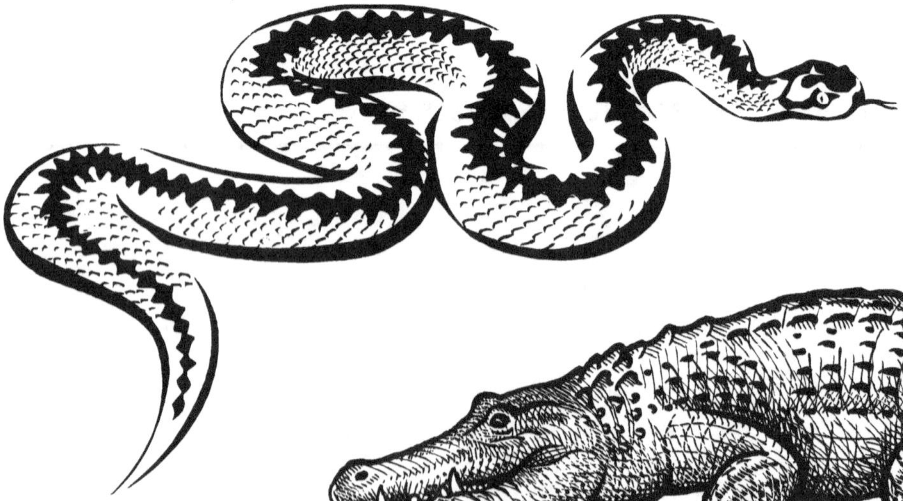
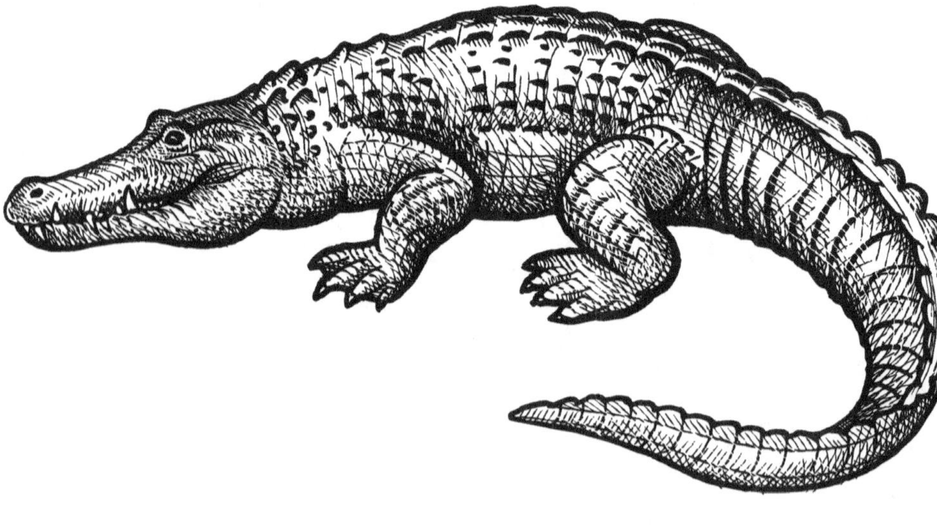
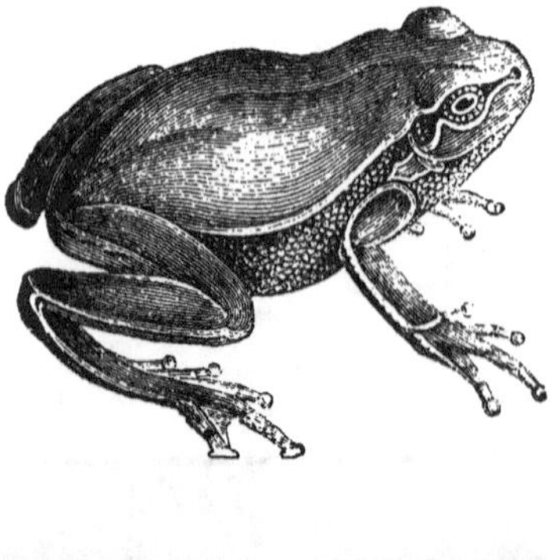

This is a

Birds

*I*f fish are considered to be the creatures of the water, then birds are the creatures of the air. Since old times, people admired the birds because they wanted to freely fly in the sky, but not all birds are able to do that. The biggest bird in the world is the African Ostrich. It can run perfectly, but it cannot get up in the air. The weight of the bird can be almost 300 pounds, so it is much bigger than a person. Even the birds' eggs can be up to 3 pounds. The smallest birds are the hummingbirds, and there are around 300 different species of them. The tiniest among them are only 2 inches in length and weigh about 0.05 ounces. The hummingbirds are called 'the pearls among the feathered'.

The feathers of a hummingbird are full of purely bright colors. They wave their wings so fast that you can't even see them. Instead, you see a little cloud around the bird and can hear a buzzing sound. These birds are like little helicopters because they can change directions really fast, hover over a flower and even fly backwards. They like to eat the nectar from plants and bugs.

Birds' bodies are covered with feathers which allow them to fly or help some of them to stay on the water's surface. Feathers can look very pretty, like the ones you see on peacocks.

- Questions:

  1. What bird isn't able to fly?

  ____

  ____

  ____

  2. What is the smallest bird called?

  ____

  ____

  ____

  3. What do hummingbirds eat?

  ____

  ____

  ____

- Draw here what you liked most about this chapter:

Some birds stay in the same region for their whole lives. Those are called winter birds. The most popular winter bird is the sparrow. It has a grey head, a brown back with wide black stripes, a tail, wings that are black and brown, and a black chin and throat. In spring, sparrows eat little bugs and caterpillars while in winter and autumn they eat the seeds of plants.

The sparrows like to live in people's houses. There, they always have food and are protected from predators. They make their nests under the roofs and under other coverings. The sparrow couples build their nests together out of feathers, cotton pieces, and straw. After that, they take turns keeping the eggs warm with their bodies in preparation for them to hatch. In two weeks, little chicks are born, and the parents spend all of their time feeding them. The sparrows bring food to their babies 300-400 times per day! Little sparrows grow up quickly, and during the summer, there can be a few generations in just one nest.

The sparrows often look for food all together. If one finds a lot of it, it starts to tweet loudly to call over its family. A group of sparrows can even win a fight with a hawk. They gather together tightly and fight the hawk all together so that it has no choice but to fly away.

- **Questions:**

    1. What are the birds that always live in one place called?

    ____
    ____
    ____

    2. What do sparrows eat in spring?

    ____
    ____
    ____

    3. Do sparrows like to live close to people?

    ____
    ____
    ____

- **Draw here what you liked most about this chapter:**

*C*rows have adjusted to life with people as well. They are very smart, contriving and sharp-witted birds. They find their food in trash cans and in big trashed areas. The crows are large and are fairly colorless. Its head, beak, throat, wings, feet, and tail are black while the rest of the body is grey. Many of the crows leave the cities in the spring, so they can go to the wooded areas to build their nests. The nests are big and are built with cotton and feathers inside of them. The mother crow takes care of her eggs, while the father crow feeds her. In two weeks, very hungry babies are born. The parents feed them first and then teach them to hunt for their own food.

Crows often destroy nests of other birds and take away their babies. They also often steal the eggs that were left. The crows don't only crow, but they can also copy some other noises like a dog's bark or a person's laugh. They like to mock dogs by sitting in trees and barking. Healthy crows sometimes take care of the sick ones by bringing them food and helping them to drink by passing water from their beaks to the others.

- Questions:

    1. Where do crows live?

    2. What colors are the crow's feathers?

    3. In what way can a crow be harmful?

- Draw here what you liked most about this chapter:

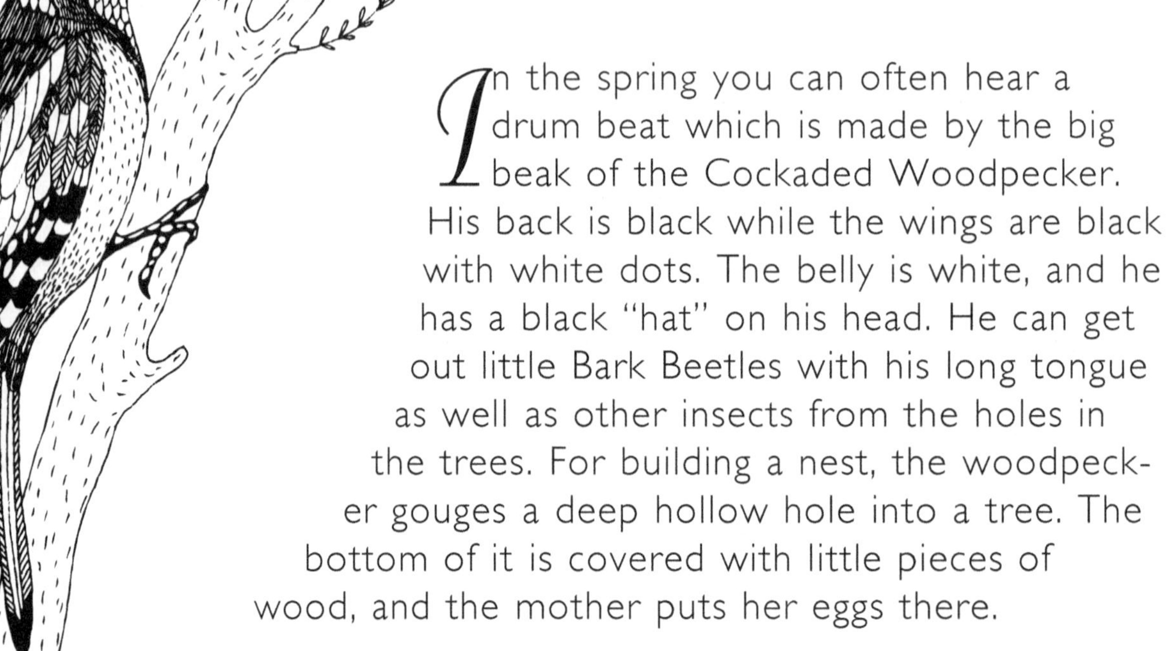

*I*n the spring you can often hear a drum beat which is made by the big beak of the Cockaded Woodpecker. His back is black while the wings are black with white dots. The belly is white, and he has a black "hat" on his head. He can get out little Bark Beetles with his long tongue as well as other insects from the holes in the trees. For building a nest, the woodpecker gouges a deep hollow hole into a tree. The bottom of it is covered with little pieces of wood, and the mother puts her eggs there.

Babies are born in the spring. They are born blind and without feathers. During winter, the woodpeckers don't go to the other countries because pine cones are enough food for them during the cold time of the year. You can easily see the place where these birds have been because the snow under a tree will be covered with little wood pieces from the eaten cones.

In our forests, you can find birds that have babies not in spring or summer, as others do, but in the cold of January instead. They are called Crossbills. The Crossbill builds deep nests with strong walls and makes them warm with cotton pads, feathers and pieces of hair so that they can keep their babies from being cold. The mother bird won't leave the nest until after the babies have grown their first feathers. Before that time comes, the father bird brings the mother food by taking out the seeds of pine cones that have grown at the end of the season. When the time gets closer to spring, the cones open up. At that point, the grown babies are able to leave the nest and get the seeds by themselves.

• Questions:

1. What is the color of a woodpecker's cap?

2. When do woodpeckers have chicks?

3. When do Crossbill chicks hatch?

• Draw here what you liked most about this chapter:

Many birds, such as doves, crows, and magpies, spend the winter in North America. Not all birds can survive cold winters like the ones that live by lakes, rivers and swamps for example. Ducks, geese, swans and cranes take a long journey to the more southern areas right before the cold hits; the grass is turning yellow, and the leaves are falling down. Before that, the birds that eat insects leave because there are not many of them before winter. These are called migratory birds, and they include swallows, cranes and many others.

- **Questions:**

  1. Name the birds that stay during winter.

  ____

  ____

  ____

  2. What birds are called migratory?

  ____

  ____

  ____

  3. What birds live on the lakes and rivers?

  ____

  ____

  ____

- **Draw here what you liked most about this chapter:**

Every bird has a job in the forest during spring. They bring little sticks, grass and pieces of moss to build nests for the next generation. In the springtime, among the reed and sedge, the grey ducks come to live. Their feathers are grayish-brownish, so it is hard to notice them when they are in the reeds and brown grass toward the end of the year. The male drakes look very fancy because they have blue and green necks and wings that sparkle in the sun, while the females are more neutral looking with their feathers having white and dark brown stripes instead. The father duck chooses a place for the nest while the mother duck covers it with cotton and feathers.

The mother lays about ten eggs and will leave the nest sometimes to eat lake grass or little plankton. During those times, the father bird swims nearby to make sure the place is safe. In three weeks time, they have little fluffy babies. The mother duck takes them to the river immediately where they jump into water fearlessly and play. After swimming, they clean up their feathers and put oil on them. It is very important because only clean and fluffy feathers can hold them above the water. Dirty feathers get sticky and can cause a duck to drown.

In the fall, the young ducks start finding mates. The female chooses a male, and they often spend their whole lives together. Ducks are the last of the birds to leave for the warm regions during winter because they have enough food until rivers and lakes start to become icy. In the cities, they often spend winter in places where the water doesn't freeze.

- Questions:

    1. What do ducks eat?

    ____
    ____
    ____

    2. Why do ducks clean their feathers?

    ____
    ____
    ____

    3. What does a mother duck teach her ducklings?

    ____
    ____
    ____

- Draw here what you liked most about this chapter:

Different birds will lay a different number of eggs. Little singing birds have the least amount being about only four or five, but the Grey Partridge has twenty simultaneously! Some birds, like sparrows, crows and doves for instance, have babies that are helpless, blind and naked when they're born. Parents bring them food, keep them warm and protect them from predators. These birds are called nestling birds. Other birds like quails, geese, ducks, and seagulls don't have babies that are blind and featherless when they're born. After they have dried, they can follow their parents and eat by themselves. These birds are called hatching. Usually, nestling birds have fewer eggs than hatching birds because the parents are not able to feed a large amount of babies.

When days become shorter and it is harder to get food, migrating birds get ready to leave. How do they find their way? Scientists believe that some birds can orienteer as well as ships and planes do by using the magnetic field of the Earth. Special organs act like miniature compasses by letting them define where north and south is. They can also find their way by the stars. This is why they don't like to fly in bad and foggy weather.

After a long, cold winter and when the weather starts to get warmer, the fields and forests get filled with the loud singing of different birds. This is why there is a saying that birds bring to us a long-awaited spring on their wings.

- Questions:

    1. How many eggs can a partridge lay?

    ____

    ____

    ____

    2. How do birds find their way when flying?

    ____

    ____

    ____

    3. Do all birds lay the same number of eggs?

    ____

    ____

    ____

- Draw here what you liked most about this chapter:

Test Yourself:

Let's check: how well do you know birds?
Write under each bird its name.

Mammals

You most likely have met mammals in the early years of your life. You could see dogs and cats in the yard, and if you ever went to a farm, you could spot horses and cows. You could also see many mammals on TV. What are mammals, and how are they different from other animals? First, the bodies of most of them is covered with fur. Second, they feed their young with milk. These are some of the distinguishing features of mammals. Mammals are the inhabitants of the Earth's surface, and many of them live in water as well. Do you think that whales and dolphins are fish? Well, guess what? They breathe air, give birth to babies and feed them with milk, so they are mammals too! There are mammals that are able to fly the air like bats or live under the ground like moles and some species of mice.

Mammals can be very little, or they can also be very big. You probably just thought of an elephant. It is the biggest animal that lives on the Earth's sur-face, but the Blue Whale is even bigger! They can be over 100 feet in length and can weigh up to 150 tons! No truck is able to pick up such a huge body, nor is there a train that is able to do that!

• Questions:

1. Name three of your favorite mammals.

____

____

____

2. What do baby mammals eat for food?

____

____

____

3. What kind of mammals live in the water?

____

____

____

• Draw here what you liked most about this chapter:

Mammals can be herbivores or predators. The herbivores eat grass, leaves, and other plants while predators eat other animals. But, don't think that the predators are able to live without plants. If plants disappeared from the earth due to some kind of accident, all of the herbivorous mammals would die too, so the predators wouldn't have anything to eat. Every living thing makes up a part of the food chain. For instance, mice eat seeds and plants, and foxes eat mice. If mice disappear, foxes will too. There are longer and more complicated food chains in nature.

You can tell a lot about an animal's life by just observing its appearance. If an animal has long and muscular legs, it means it is a good runner. Such animals, like deer and wild horses, run away to save themselves from predators, and predators have to run even faster to get to their prey. The fastest runner is the cheetah, and it can run at a speed of 65-75 mi/hr. If an animal has long back legs, it means that it moves by jumping, like a hare or a squirrel. The squirrel has nails on its paws, so it can climb trees very well while some monkeys have long tails to help them jump from tree to tree or even hang on them.

- Questions:

1. What two groups are mammals divided into?

2. Up to what speeds can a cheetah run?

3. What do mice eat?

- Draw here what you liked most about this chapter:

The colors of animals often depend on the area where they live. Herbivores hide from their enemies and predators want to get to them by not being noticed which allows them to get as close to them as possible. This type of coloring scheme is called camouflage. Animals that live in a desert, like camels, have a yellowish-brown color so they can look the same as the sand. A tiger is hard to notice because of the dark black and orange coloring on its fur. A polar bear is white because it hunts among the ice and snow. People made up masking equipment and clothes so they are harder to notice in either the snow covered forest or the green leaves and grass.

Some animals' fur color changes depending on the season. The hare changes his fur every fall by turning from brown to white so that it can hide better in the snow. Squirrels become silvery-grey from being golden red. While changing color, the fur also becomes thicker and warmer.

- Questions:

    1. What is protective color scheming called?

    ____

    ____

    ____

    2. What is the color of a hare's fur in winter?

    ____

    ____

    ____

    3. What is the color of a squirrel's fur in winter?

    ____

    ____

    ____

- Draw here what you liked most about this chapter:

Now, the mammals are getting ready for winter. During this time, certain animals, like reindeer, will migrate south where it is easier to find food. Since reindeer are a main food source for the wolves, they migrate with them too. Many herbivorous animals, such as sheep, elk and deer, spend the summer on high hills full of tasty grass and then go down to the valleys during the winter where the snow isn't as deep. Many of the larger mammals get into big groups for winter. Wolves, on the other hand, stay in packs all year round because it's the easiest way for them to hunt bigger prey such deer, elk or wild boar. Usually, wolves primarily hunt for weak or sick animals which is why they are sometimes referred to as "forest doctors".

Many animals store up food supplies for winter. Beavers cut and gather fallen tree branches and the roots of water plants. A family of beavers can store over 700 cubic feet of food supplies for the winter. Mice bring seeds and acorns to their burrow while squirrels put them carefully into the big hollows of trees. Hedgehogs and some other animals don't need to store supplies because they go into hibernation (a long sleep) until spring comes.

- Questions:

  1. What do some animals store for winter?

  ____
  ____
  ____

  2. What does a hedgehog do during winter?

  ____
  ____
  ____

  3. Why are wolves sometimes called "forest doctors"?

  ____
  ____
  ____

- Draw here what you liked most about this chapter:

Wild animals have been used as a food source for people for thousands of years. But, food isn't the only use for wild animals. Almost every single part can be used for other purposes such as clothing, blankets or even weapons. We get our honey from bees. For thousands of years, people have tamed a variety of animals. Some of them, such as horses, donkeys, camels, and deer, are used for hard, physical labor such as pulling wagons, being ridden or carrying things. Others give us products that are essential for life. For example, cows and goats give milk, and chickens provide eggs. Some wonderful materials can be made from the furs of sheep or camels. Dogs help us out too by protecting our homes and other facilities, finding criminals, searching and rescuing people from destroyed buildings after a disaster or even finding people who get lost in the mountains. Along with cats, dogs are also faithful friends to many people. It's hard to imagine the existence of our society without our beloved pets.

- Questions:

    1. Name some animals that do hard, physical work.

    ____

    ____

    ____

    2. What useful thing do cows and goats give us?

    ____

    ____

    ____

    3. How do dogs help us?

    ____

    ____

    ____

- Draw here what you liked most about this chapter:

Test Yourself:

Let's check: How well do you know animals?
Write under each mammal its name.

Natural Zones

Nature conditions in parts of the world can be very different from each other. Scientists have divided the territories with similar climates, vegetation and its inhabitants. These territories are called the Natural Zones. In America, there are six main natural zones: the Tundra, the Taiga, the Forest, the Prairie, the Desert, and the Flooded Grasslands.

The Arctic Desert

The Arctic Desert is an area of infinite snow. For almost the whole year, the Arctic Ocean is covered with ice. Polar nights last long for months, and the only thing coloring the sky is the Aurora Borealis. During the short summer, polar days are only for a few weeks, and there is no darkness at all. Although the sun doesn't leave the sky during the evening, it doesn't rise above the horizon which prevents the ground from warming up. For a small window of time the snow melts exposing the rocky ground. In these conditions, plants are not able to exist, however there is plenty of food in the sea. Every year, thousands of nestling birds such as Seagulls, Polar Terns, Cleavers, Guillemots, Eiders and Barring Cormorants migrate from the warmer countries to the rocky coasts. Huge bird colonies sit on the unassailable cliff ledges and make very loud noises. These colonies are called "Birds' Bazaar". Even though polar summers are very short, it is the prime time for taking care of eggs and babies which is why the polar birds sleep for only for 1-2 hours per day. The birds take out their own feathers to make a covering for their babies so they don't freeze. People gather these feathers and make special warm and light outfits for polar explorers, mountain climbers and anyone else who lives in the cold, northern parts of the world. Some animals have adapted to survive in that harsh part of the world. In the Far North, there is almost no permanent population. In general, scientific stations are built here where scientists study the weather, the animals, and search for minerals.

The Polar Bear

The White Polar Bear got its name because of the white fur that it has, but is also simply known as the Polar Bear, the Northern Bear, or the Sea Bear. The Polar Bear is one of the predator mammals of the bear family. This is a big animal with a long neck and flat head. It has strong legs, its feet are covered in fur, and it has swimming membranes between its toes.

The fur on the feet keeps the paws warm on the ice and keeps the bear from slipping. The bear's skin is actually black, but its fur is white. The white fur helps it to hide in the snow, and the black skin attracts the sunlight which also aids in keeping the bear warm. At the time of polar summer, the fur gets a little yellowish. The hairs within the fur are empty inside, and they hold in air to also keep the bear feeling warm in its coat along with the big layer of fat found beneath its coat. Underneath the coat is a big layer of fat. The polar bear lives in the arctic region that has moving ice within the northern seas. People call the polar bear "The Host of the Arctic". A polar bear can run and swim very well, and it hunts fish, seals, sea hares and walruses.

Polar bears make dens in the snow that they sleep in. At the end of the arctic winter, the mother bear has one to three cubs. The cubs stay in the den while the mother feeds them with her milk. When the cubs grow up, they leave their den and start wandering around with their mother where she teaches them how to hunt and hide from enemies.

• Questions:

1. Why is the polar bear also called white polar bear?

2. Where does the polar bear live?

3. Where does the polar bear hunt?

• Draw here what you liked most about this chapter:

The Walrus

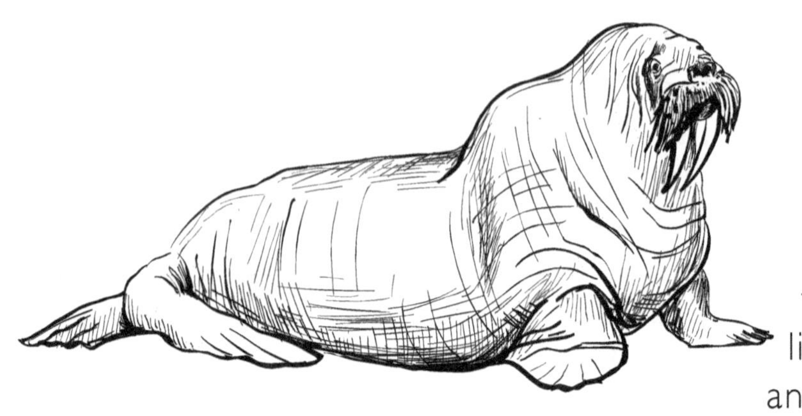

The Walrus is a mammal from the Pinniped group. It has a massive body and a small head. Its long, hard moustache is easily noticed on the wide face that it has, and its little eyes are set far from one another. It has huge fangs for digging the ground underwater in order to get mollusks, for protecting himself from enemies, and for climbing onto the ice when it gets out of the water.

The males have big bumps on the skin called warts. Under the skin, there is a big amount of fat that helps the walrus deal with the cold climate. It doesn't have much hair, but the hair it does have is red. The older the walrus is, the less hair it has. Their flippers help them to easily swim and move along the ground. The walrus lives on the coasts of the cold seas of the northern half of the world. With loud screaming, they warn all of the others of danger. When they hear it, the whole group flees to the sea because that is where they feel the most comfortable. Did you know that walruses can sleep underwater?

A mother gives birth to only one baby and feeds it milk for a long time. It takes care of the baby very well and protects it from enemies. If the baby can't get down to the water, she pushes it, and if it's tired, she puts it on her back and gives it a ride. When the baby has its own fangs, it's considered an adult and will then start hunting on its own. The walrus eats mollusks, worms, crustaceans and fish. Their enemies are polar bears and orcas (killer whales), but the main enemy of this animal are human beings.

- Questions:

1. Where does the walrus live?

2. When is the walrus considered an adult?

3. What are the enemies of the walrus?

- Draw here what you liked most about this chapter:

The Seal

There are many kinds of seals: the greenlandic seal, the striped seal, the sea hare, the sea leopard and others. These animals are mammals. The seal has a big body that's shaped like a ship, and it has flippers with claws on them. This body build lets the animal swim and dive very well. They have short fur that can be white, grey or black shades. Under their skin is a big layer of fat that helps the animals survive in harsh conditions. They eat fish and crustaceans. When they are hunting in the water, they demonstrate great dexterity and speed, but you can't say that about them when they are on land.

The seals live in cold regions next to the North Pole and come together as families making "seal beds". In such gatherings they give birth to their babies. Every mother can only have one pup at a time. Baby seals are completely white and have long, thick fur. The mother feeds it with milk and hides it from enemies such as polar bears. In some time, the baby starts to molt its fur.

When the baby becomes the color of the adults, it starts an independent life. Since old times, people hunted seals to eat their meat and fat and use their skins, but now it is forbidden to hunt them in many areas.

• Questions:

   1. What do seals eat?

   2. How many babies can a mother seal have?

   3. Who is the enemy of the seals?

• Draw here what you liked most about this chapter:

The Blue Whale

The blue whale is the biggest mammal on our planet, and it got the name "blue" because of the color of its skin. Sometimes it is called the blue whale and sometimes it's called the big striped whale because the lengthwise folds on its belly look like stripes. On the outside, the whale looks like big fish, but it is not a fish, it is a mammal that breathes with its lungs and has a body temperature of about 100 degrees Fahrenheit. The blue whale has a mouth called a baleen, and it needs it to eat. The whale opens its mouth wide and swims forward. While it does this, little fish, crustaceans and mollusks are captured into its mouth and get stuck in the baleen where horned discs hang just like a sieve.

All that the whale has to do is close its mouth to gather food with its gigantic tongue. This animal needs to eat a ton of little animals to get full. Usually, the whales stay in small groups of about 2 or 3. They can swim very well, and they like to dive and make loud, noisy fountains with their blowholes. Once every two years, the female gives birth to an enormous baby and feeds it with milk that has ten times as much fat as a cow's milk. The baby grows very fast, and it can gain up to 220 pounds per day! Blue whales live both in the northern and southern seas, but they only give birth in warmer bodies of water. A long time ago, there were a lot more whales than there are today. Whalers killed a big number of the whales for their baleens, and they used them for making brushes, horsewhips and corsages for ladies. The whale's meat was used as food while the fat was used to make butter, soap and oil for lamps. Unfortunately, the blue whale is on the extinction list now.

- Questions:

1. Why is the blue whale called blue?

____

____

____

2. How does this whale gather its food?

____

____

____

3. Why is the blue whale on the endangered list?

____

____

____

- Draw here what you liked most about this chapter:

The Tundra

The tundra ranges over 300 miles along the coast of the Arctic Ocean. The ground there melts down only during the short summer period, but under the water, it is infinitely frozen. This naturally treeless area stretches in the subarctic zone. The climate there is severe with prolonged cold winters (-510 F to -690 F) and short, cool summers (up to -148 F). Freezing soil and rocks form what's called permafrost as a result. Due to lack of heat, trees do not grow in the tundra. The animal world of the tundra is not very rich. The common animals are reindeer, the artic fox, lemmings, the white partridge and the white owl. The waterfowl ranges from geese, ducks, swans to loons. The plants found here are common mosses and lichens, sedge, cranberries, dwarf birch and alder bushes. The plants grow on slopes in order to withstand strong winds.

Reindeer

The reindeer is an artiodactyls mammal of the deer family. This is a big animal with branchy antlers and wide hooves. The whole body of the deer is covered with thick, warm fur. The color of fur in summer is brown while it turns grey in winter. The reindeer are herd animals, so they get into big herds and travel long distances looking for food. At the end of summer, the mothers have one or two babies. The baby stays with the mother for two years. She feeds it milk and protects it from predators such as wolves and other carnivorous animals.

- Questions:

   1. What color of fur does a reindeer have in summer?

   2. Why reindeer they get into big herds?

   3. What is an enemy to the reindeer?

- Draw here what you liked most about this chapter:

Arctic Fox

The arctic fox is a small predatory mammal of the dog family. Sometimes, it is called a polar fox. It really looks like a fox, but it is a little shorter. The arctic fox has a short muzzle, little round ears and very beautiful fur that changes just like the fur of a hare does. In winter, it is white and shiny and a dark bluish color in the summer. The bottom of its paws, heels and toes are covered with thick fur that protects the arctic fox from the cold. It lives in the tundra, behind the Arctic Circle. They dig burrows with many corridors on the little hills.

Sometimes, a few families live in these labyrinths. The burrows are used for many years because, in the tundra, there aren't many hills that can be used for living in. The arctic foxes are very fertile. A mother can give birth to up to ten cubs at a time. The cubs sit in the shelters quietly while their parents warn them about coming dangers with their loud barking.

The cubs grow up very fast and soon start hunting by themselves. The arctic fox eats lemmings, mice, birds, seaweed and fish. Such enemies like other foxes, wolverines, wolves, and even polar owls will hunt the cubs. Besides the reindeer and arctic foxes, there are also white hares, lemmings and weasels living in the tundra region, and sometimes foxes and wolves go there too. Their warm fur saves them from the cold winters. There are many birds such as geese, seagulls and scabs on the lakes filled with fish in summer. It is there that they give birth to their babies, but the only ones spending winter in the tundra are the white owls and polar partridges.

- **Questions:**

   1. What animals live in the tundra?

   ____

   ____

   ____

   2. What does the arctic fox eat?

   ____

   ____

   ____

   3. What are the enemies of the arctic fox?

   ____

   ____

   ____

- **Draw here what you liked most about this chapter:**

The Forest

The forest is the biggest zone in our country. They take up a lot of space from north to south and from east to west. In the north, the forests are found along the rivers and on the little islands in the tundra region and make up an endless area of the taiga. Further south are mixed forests where Coniferous trees are mixed with birches, asps, ash and lime trees. Then, there are foliar forests with oak and maple coppices. For the whole year there is food for the animals in the forests such as mushrooms, berries, grass, acorns, cones, seeds, young trees, bushes and branches. Because of that, there are many animals, birds and insects living in the forest. The forests give us shade and cool breathes of air on hot days as they fill the air with oxygen. Because forests take up a third of the land, they are called "The lungs of the Earth".

The Bear

The bear is also called the host of the forest. Common characteristics of modern bears include large bodies with stocky legs, long snouts, small rounded ears, shaggy hair, splayed paws with five claws and short tails. It walks slowly and confidently around its area which is different from what the other animals do. In the summer and fall you can see them on the fields and glades eating chestnuts, wild pears and beech nuts. Because of the large amounts of plants it eats, it almost never hunts big animals.

Several bear species are dangerous to humans, especially in areas where they have become used to people; elsewhere, they generally avoid humans. Injuries caused by bears are rare, but are widely reported. Bears may attack humans in response to being startled, defending their young or food, or even for predatory reasons.

• Questions:

1. Write the names of a few trees that you know of in a forest.

____

____

____

2. What food can bears find in the woods?

____

____

____

3. Why may bears attack humans?

____

____

____

• Draw here what you liked most about this chapter:

The Deer

The spotted deer is a big hoofed animal and has a beautiful neck with a not so big head. Its ears are big and very flexible. The antlers have branches, and the adult males usually have about four of them. In the summer, the deer's fur is orange with white spots while in the winter, it is brownish-grey with almost no spots. The spotted deer live in the deciduous forests with thick bushes. They like the areas with oak trees, but in the winter, you can see them in the pine forests. The deer live individually or in little groups seeking shelter within the thick forest. They eat grassy plants, fallen acorns, nuts, fruit, leaves of trees, bushes, mushrooms and berries. In the winter, they also like to eat bark and young branches.

In the summer, mothers give birth to one baby at a time, which she raises up till the next spring. The deer have enemies such as wolves, foxes and humans. People will hunt them or raise them on farms and use their antlers for medicine. Some people also get milk, meat and fur from deer.

• **Questions:**

1. What do deer eat?

2. What do people get from deer?

3. Do you like the deer?

• **Draw here what you liked most about this chapter:**

The Moose

The moose is the biggest animal of the deer family. It has a big chest, short neck, long legs and a tall, hump-like back. When a moose drinks water, it goes into the deep parts and gets on its knees. It has a pretty big head with an aquiline nose with an overhang and fleshy upper lip. The fur is brown and sometimes almost black whereas the legs are almost white. The females don't have antlers, but the males have very big ones. The moose loses its horns every year at the end of fall which is also the same time when the males have their fights. They live in the forests and thick bushes on the riverbanks. It is important that there are, rivers or lakes because the moose likes to eat water plants.

In the summer, they eat grass, branches with leaves, bark, moss and mushrooms. In the winter, they eat branches and tree bark. The moose likes to go to places where salt is found because they really like to lick the salt.

In the spring, mothers give birth to one or two babies. They grow up so quickly that they can confidently stand on the second day and follow their mothers around while eating plants on the tenth day. Moose hunting is forbidden. People create moose farms where they can feed them, cure them of diseases and even milk them. The moose's milk tastes like cow's milk, but it is fattier and less sweet and can be used for medical nourishment.

• Questions:

1. Why do people create moose farms?

____

____

____

2. What color of fur does a moose have?

____

____

____

3. Where does the moose live?

____

____

____

• Draw here what you liked most about this chapter:

The Wild Boar

Wild boars are part of the pig family. Unlike the house pig, the boar has a short body and tall legs. Its head is longer and thinner and the ears are longer and pointed. The boar has strong and sharp fangs, and its course hair makes a little mane on its back. The bristles are dark brown with a black and yellow shade. The boar lives in swampy areas among trees and bushes. Females and young males live in herds while the old males live separately. The females give birth to striped babies. The stripes help them hide in the forest. The mothers take care of the babies and protect them from enemies.

Boars are clumsy, but they run and swim wonderfully. They can't see very well but have great hearing and sense of smell. They are also nocturnal meaning that they are active at night while they go out to swim or find food. During the day, they hide out in their dug up holes in the groung.

Boars eat mostly plants (roots, fruits, acorns, etc.) as well as different little animals both living and dead. They often hurt trees and agriculture such as potato, turnip and grain fields as they dig up the ground and trample on the seeds.

• Questions

1. What does the wild boar eat?

2. How do boars hurt nature?

3. What kind of fangs does the boar have?

• Draw here what you liked most about this chapter:

The Lynx

The lynx is a big animal of the cat family. It has a short tail known as a bobbed tail, pompous side-whiskers and long hair on the ears. Its body is short and has long, strong legs with wide, furry paws. The lynx's fur is either grey or reddish with dark spots. It lives in the forest and tundra regions across Canada and Alaska as well as some parts of the northern United States. It really likes coniferous and mixed forests. The lynx is a night animal and is very good at climbing trees (just like every other cat). It likes to hunt by looking for its prey from a covering, and it hunts for hares, mice, foxes and partridges. The lynx's developed sense of smell and hearing helps it when hunting even from very long distances. Usually, the weak and sick animals come to be prey of the lynx which is why it is considered as a regulator of the number of hares and other rodents in the area. The lynx's main enemy is the wolf.

In the winter, the lynx leaves big prints in the snow because their feet have a lot of long fur on them which make them bigger causing them to leave bigger foot prints. A mother lynx can give birth from two to five kittens in her den. They make their shelters under fallen trees or in their hollows. The mother feeds and takes care of the kittens for a whole year. When they are grown enough, the kittens go hunting with their mother to learn all of the secrets of catching prey.

- **Questions:**

  1. What regions does the lynx live in?

  ____

  ____

  ____

  2. Who is the enemy of the lynx?

  ____

  ____

  ____

  3. How many kittens can a mother lynx give birth to?

  ____

  ____

  ____

- **Draw here what you liked most about this chapter:**

The Hare

The hare is a forest animal, and it is not very big. Its head is relatively big and wide with long ears. The color of the hares' fur often changes. In the summer, it is either brown or red, and it turns white in the wintertime. The hare lives in the taiga and the mixed forests because there is a lot of grass there. The hare is a nocturnal animal, so it sleeps during the day. At night, it eats different plants and mushrooms. The hares have big families. A few times during the summer, a mother can have babies and usually has five or six each time. The baby hares, called leverets, are born with the ability to see, and they are covered with fur and can move around. After giving birth, the mother hare feeds the babies and then leaves them. When the left leverets become hungry, they start to move and leave their scent behind them.

Their mothers, or any other mother hare, finds them by the smell and feeds them. If the mother hare feels like there is danger, she pretends to be wounded and leads the predator far away from the babies. This is how she protects them. In the forest, under the branches of fallen trees, there live a few other animals in burrows such as badgers and foxes. While beavers make dams on the river, in the depths of the forest you can even meet a bear. In the trees' hollows you can find squirrels, martens, stoats and other different kinds of birds such as owls, eagle-owls and woodpeckers.

- Questions:

  1. What regions does the hare live in?

  ____
  ____
  ____

  2. How do mother hares protect their young?

  ____
  ____
  ____

  3. Write the names of a few animals that live in a forest.

  ____
  ____
  ____

- Draw here what you liked most about this chapter:

The Prairies

The prairies are situated to the south from the forests. In the beginning, the forests thin out and break up into small groves. Going further out, the trees start to be only found along rivers and little villages. Around them there are enormous areas covered with a variety of grass called prairies. In the summer, the days in the prairies are long and very hot whereas in the winter they are short and cold. There are many rodents that live in the prairies such as hamsters, mice and gophers. Snakes such as the coluber and steppe adder and big predator birds such as the harrier, eagle and kite are hunting the rodents. At night, the owls are hunting too. Stoats, badgers and foxes like to eat rodents as well. There are not many big herbivorous mammals in the prairies, but most often there are flocks of pronghorn (American antelope) that are looking for lush pastures.

The Wolf

The wolf is a predator of the dog family and is the ancestor of the common house dog. The wolves that live in the forest are grey whereas the wolves that live in the snowy tundra are almost white in color, and the prairie wolves (coyotes) are red. These ancient hunters can make different sounds. They can growl, roar, whine, bark and howl, and this is how they "talk" with each other and warn one another about danger that is coming. They hunt a variety deer, elk, wild boar, antelope, hares and other animals. In the spring, the mothers birth a few blind, fluffy pups.

- Questions

1. What sounds does a wolf make?

____

____

____

2. What color of fur does a coyote have?

____

____

____

3. What other facts would you add about the wolf?

____

____

____

- Draw here what you liked most about this chapter:

The Groundhog

The groundhog is a member of the marmot squirrel family. It is a small animal with a short, fluffy tail and strong paws with claws. The groundhog digs very complicated burrows with many exits using their paws and sharp teeth. In the depth of the burrows, the groundhog builds a nest and puts dry grass and leaves in it. It sleeps for the whole winter in that little warm place. The groundhog runs very fast and often poses like a pole by getting onto its back paws and looks around. It is active in the daytime and sleeps at night. The groundhog eats leaves, flowers, grain plants and different insects. In the spring time, it wakes up from hibernation and reproduces. The mother gives birth anywhere from two to seven babies and feeds them with her milk. Within a month, the young groundhogs grow up enough to eat harder foods. They can also whistle very loud which is how they communicate with each other.

• Questions

1. Where does the groundhog build its nest?

2. Where does the groundhog sleep for the whole winter?

3. What does the roundhog eat?

• Draw here what you liked most about this chapter:

The Desert

Farther south, the prairies turn into deserts. The North American xeric region is over 95,751 sq miles and includes three major deserts, numerous smaller deserts, and large, non-desert arid regions within the western United States and in northeast, central, and northwest Mexico. Rain doesn't fall very often in the desert, and the hot sun dries up the soil. The air temperature can get up to 140 degrees Fahrenheit, and the soil can get up to 194 degrees Fahrenheit, so it becomes a natural frying pan. The biggest treasure in the desert is water. It is there, but it's hidden deep under the ground in the water preserving layers. In the places where it is close to the surface, beautiful oases appear. They are full of pompous looking and juicy plants. In the daytime, it is very hot in the desert, but it becomes freezing cold during the night. The reason for that is because there is a very little amount of moisture in the air which is supposed to keep it warm at night. Many animals live at nighttime and hide in cool burrows during the hot day. The daytime animals go out early in the morning. Desert animals are able to get their water from plants and preserve it for long periods of time in their bodies.

The Puma

The puma (mountain lion) is a common member of the Felidae family, native to all of the Americas. They range from the Canadian Yukon to the southern Andes of South America. In various regions, they are also known as panthers. Within the desert regions of North America, they are the most dominant predator. They can reach speeds of 50 mph in a sprint, leap 15 feet high into a tree, easily scale a 12-foot-tall fence and can maintain a speed of 10 mph for many miles. A male mountain lion can weigh up to 180 pounds.

The sounds that puma makes are also more similar to those of small felines than the roars of the big cats. They communicate through growls, chirps and whistles. Pumas are good at climbing trees, which helps them to get out escape bigger predators like jaguars and bears that sometimes share their habitat.

- Questions:

  1. What other names of puma?

  ____
  ____
  ____

  2. What sounds does puma make?

  ____
  ____
  ____

  3. What other facts can you say about the puma?

  ____
  ____
  ____

- Draw here what you liked most about this chapter:

The Antelope

The antelope is an Artiodactyla mammal of the Parietal family. In the Greek translation, the word "antelope" means an animal with horns. There are a few kinds of antelope ranging from very small to as big as a bull. They can have either straight horns or wavy ones like the grazing antelope. There are even others with curled ones such as the nyala antelopes. Within this species, there is also a variety of fur color and shape. One of the most beautiful types of antelopes is the bongo. It is large in size with a beautiful head and long horns that look like spirals. The length of the male's horns can be up to three feet in length. They have a short manes on their backs, and their fur is bright brown and orange with white stripes on their sides. Although beautiful, people must use caution when around the bongo antelope.

A female antelope gives birth to one baby every year and feeds it with milk and hides it from enemies in thick bushes and long grass.

• Questions:

1. Name a couple of kinds of antelope.

2. What is the most beautiful type of antelope?

3. Which breed of antelope should you use caution?

• Draw here what you liked most about this chapter:

The Coyote

The coyote is a predatory mammal of the dog family. The word "coyote" translates as "the godly dog". Sometimes it is called the lawn wolf or prairie wolf. It is smaller than a regular sized wolf but looks a lot like it. The coyote has a strong, thick body, standing ears, a long, fluffy tail and mighty legs. Its fur is long and brown with black spots. The belly is lighter in color, and the end of its tail is black. The coyotes live in pairs or in packs. Each pack has its own territory and protects it from unwanted enemies. The coyotes are true hunters, and they can run fast while going very long distances. They hunt raccoons, rabbits, beavers, ferrets and opossums. Sometimes, they consider eating lizards and frogs.

These animals also like berries and nuts. The coyotes are wonderful singers. They howl loudly where everyone around the area can hear them very well. They form very strong bonds with their mates, and they make their shelter in a cave or an old burrow.

Mother coyotes give birth to up to ten pups at a time, and both of the parents take part in feeding and raising them. The main enemies of coyotes are pumas and wolves. Despite that, the number of coyotes is increasing lately because they are able to adjust to different life conditions.

• **Questions:**

1. What does a coyote look like?

2. Where does a coyote hunt?

3. What are the enemies of the coyotes?

• **Draw here what you liked most about this chapter:**

The Flooded Grasslands

*I*n North America, the flooded grasslands are commonly known as the wetlands or as swamps. These areas are dominated by trees and woody bushes rather than grasses and low herbs. These grasslands have innumerable values within nature by providing habitats for a great number of flora and fauna. It aids in recharging, discharging and purifying the water, and it adds to the human wonder of nature. Nonetheless, they have often been looked at as useless wastelands and even as dangerous ones that spread diseases. As a result, many people have drained or otherwise altered these lands in order to be converted for residential, industrial or agricultural use. Today, there is a greater awareness of their value which has heightened protection of these unique areas.

The Alligator

Alligators, despite their fierce reputation and appearance, are reasonably easy going creatures (not to be confused with their snappier and more aggressive relatives, the crocodile). Alligators can withstand dramatic drops in temperature and can even remain locked in ice for up to three weeks with just a small breathing hole, and it will slow its body functions to virtually shut down. When the alligators bellow, you can hear them echoing across the swamplands. As one begins, others take up the call until dozens of them are doing it. Only the males bellow by giving out a deep, throaty rumble, and although it can happen at any time of year, it's more common during the mating season.

The American alligator can lay 10 to 50 eggs at a time. After the hard-shelled eggs are laid, the mother alligator will cover them with more mud, sticks and plants. Alligators may eat fish, mollusks, birds, small mammals and other reptiles. Though carnivores usually only eat meat, alligators will also munch on fruit.

- Questions:

1. With which animal can you confuse the alligator?

2. How long can an alligator remain locked in ice?

3. Who makes the deep, loud bellowing noises: males or females?

- Draw here what you liked most about this chapter:

The Mayfly

Billions of mayflies hatch every year on the Mississippi River, and each one lives for only one day. Even so, there are so many that they actually provide food for an enormous range of animals in and around the water. Hatching isn't always predictable, but here's what we do know: for two hours every night, like clockwork, the new hatchlings take to the air as the females, who hatched the night before, dance back onto the river to lay their eggs. This is their last act before dying. These eggs will sink into the river and develop into naiads, the immature stage of the mayfly, which will live in the water up to a year before emerging. Mayflies will only hatch in clean water, so when they hatch in large numbers, it's a sign that the fish in that area are healthy.

• **Questions:**

1. What is the name of the river where billions of mayflies hatch every year?

____

____

____

2. How long is the immature stage of the mayfly where they live in the water before emerging?

____

____

____

3. What type of water do the mayfly eggs hatch in? Clean or dirty?

____

____

____

• **Draw here what you liked most about this chapter:**

The Jaguar

Jaguars are among the most elusive and secretive of the big cats. Their usual diet consists of peccaries (wild pigs), tapirs and monkeys. Their absolute favorite, however, is the adult olive ridley turtle. These turtles are an easy target for the cats because their powerful jaws can crack the protective shell as if it were a nut, and they are an ideal food source. The jaguar's hunting style is unique because they will stalk their prey before pouncing and dragging it into the cover of the trees. Once the kill is made, the jaguar will return to its kill over a period of days.

Baby jaguar are born blind, deaf and helpless. Jaguar mothers find a den an underground burrow, under a thick patch of plants or a cleft in the rocks to give birth. The mother vigorously defends her cubs. She nurses them until they are between 3 and 5 months old.

• Questions:

1. What is the jaguar's usual diet?

____

____

____

2. Why is the jaguar's hunting style unique?

____

____

____

3. Why do you like the jaguar? Write below:

____

____

____

• Draw here what you liked most about this chapter:

Epilogue

There are more than four thousand different kinds of animals on Earth. There is no such thing as a useless animal because every kind plays their own role in living nature. Despite that, each year there are fewer and fewer animals in the world. People are destroying nature more and more, and for the animals, especially the bigger ones, there are less and less untouched areas left to live in. Many kinds of animals might become extinct in the next few years. This doesn't just exhaust nature, but it also ruins the balance that was made from the beginning of time. When the predators disappear, nothing can control the amount of smaller rodents such as mice which ruin fields and destroy stored food supplies. Only people are able to save the rare kinds of animals on this planet, and it will allow nature to continue delighting us with its variety and beauty. You can help nature as well, and it is very simple to do. There is no need to trash the forest, break tree branches, cut trees down, get forest flowers, or harm animals. Remember that nature is your home too. Love it, and it will love you back.

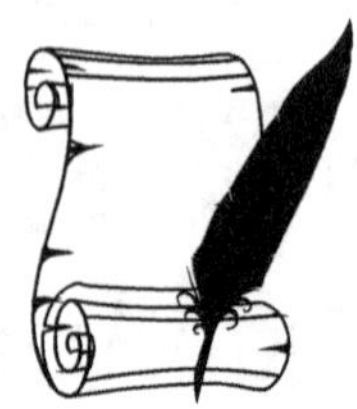

The Amazing World of the Wild
Series of Books About the Wild volume 1
North America

Insects, birds, fish, amphibians, reptiles, mammals, and other inhabitants in their natural Environment
Provided are illustrations, questions and exercises that are created from the educational discoveries within this handbook. These activities are formulated for children 8-12 years old.

Author: Anna Zubrytska
Editor: Amanda Walker
Designer: Feodor Zubrytsky

Fun Book for Kids and Their Parents
www.funbookforkids.com

www.ingramcontent.com/pod-product-compliance
Lightning Source LLC
Chambersburg PA
CBHW081619250726
48657CB00009B/2632